Is Jesus God?

Examining the Evidence

by
Adrian Lickorish

*All booklets are published thanks to the
generous support of the members of the
Catholic Truth Society*

CATHOLIC TRUTH SOCIETY

PUBLISHERS TO THE HOLY SEE

Contents

Introduction 3

Did Jesus live at all? 5

Are the Gospel authors trustworthy? 11

How were the Gospels compiled? 17

Have the Gospels been passed down to us accurately? . . .21

Does archeology support the Gospels? 25

What does Truth look like? .29

The cultural background 34

How did Jesus describe himself? 36

Understanding Jesus through his actions 44

The Resurrection 48

The conduct of the Apostles. 57

The belief of the early Church 60

The judgement of history 68

Conclusions 72

First published 2016 by The Incorporated Catholic Truth Society 40-46 Harleyford Road London SE11 5AY Tel: 020 7640 0042 Fax: 020 7640 0040 © 2016 Adrian Lickorish. This edition © 2016 The Incorporated Catholic Truth Society. The Bible quotations in this booklet are taken from The New Jerusalem Bible. Images: Page 6, Christ mosaic in the Golgotha chapel at the Church of the Holy Sepulchre /Godong / UIG / Bridgeman Images. Page 22, Page from the Codex Sinaiticus, Egypt / Photo © Zev Radovan / Bridgeman Images. Page 47, The Incredulity of Thomas / Davis Museum and Cultural Center, USA / Bridgeman Images.

ISBN 978 178469 097 7

Introduction

I believe in one Lord Jesus Christ,
The only begotten Son of God,
Born of the Father before all ages.
God from God, light from light,
True God from true God,
Begotten, not made, consubstantial with the Father.
                                    (The Nicene Creed)[1]

Christians come in all shapes and sizes, with different beliefs and practices, conduct and interests. But there is one constant: if you are a Christian, you believe that Jesus is God, one of the three persons of the Trinity.

Is that a reasonable belief? Can someone of good intelligence, open mind and enquiring spirit, acquire, hold and defend that belief today?

The burden of this booklet is that there are powerful reasons and convincing evidence, readily understood, to support the belief that Jesus is God, one of the three persons of the Trinity.

A succinct summary of the reasons and evidence, with sufficient detail to allow the reader to form a view, is set out here. The books which the author found helpful, setting out the material in far greater depth and detail, are listed under Bibliography and Further reading.

This booklet concentrates on the divinity of Jesus. Reasons of space and focus mean that it deliberately does not seek to extend its scope to an examination of the concept of the Trinity.

Did Jesus live at all?

Not even the Jewish and pagan antagonists who attacked Christianity and Jesus himself entertained the thought that he never existed.

(Bart D. Ehrman)[2]

From time to time since the eighteenth century (and not infrequently today) someone suggests that Jesus never lived. He is a myth. A figure like King Arthur or Robin Hood, encapsulating hopes and dreams, but of no reality.

The answer is that there is clear evidence, from *outside* Christian sources, that Jesus did exist at the time claimed by the New Testament. The evidence records Jesus as a teacher and miracle worker, who was crucified under Pilate and whose followers regarded him as Christ.

Josephus

Josephus was a Jew, a Pharisee, an author, a man who worked closely with the Romans, a man who knew and was a pensioner of the Emperor Vespasian. Josephus was born in AD 37 and died about AD 100. One of his works is the *Antiquities of the Jewish People*, completed in about AD 93 (about two years before the Apostle John's death). In this work Josephus makes two references to Jesus.

The shorter reads:

> [The high priest Ananias] "convened the judges of the Sanhedrin and brought before them a man named James, the brother of Jesus, who was called the Christ, and certain others. He accused them of having transgressed the law and delivered them up to be stoned."[3]

The longer reference reads:

About this time arose Jesus, a wise man [if indeed it be right to call him a man]. For he was a doer of marvellous deeds, and a teacher of men who gladly receive the truth. He drew to himself many persons, both of the Jews and of the Gentiles. [He was the Christ]. And when Pilate, upon the indictment of the leading men among us, had condemned him to the cross, those who had loved him at the first did not cease to do so, [for he appeared to them alive on the third day - the godly prophets having foretold these and ten thousand other wonderful things about him]. And even to this day the race of Christians, who are named from him, has not died out.[4]

The words in square brackets are of uncertain authenticity. Even disregarding them, the extract is evidence for Jesus as a teacher, a "doer of marvellous deeds", with followers before and after his death, who was crucified under Pilate.

Pliny the Younger

Pliny the Younger (c. AD 62-113) was the governor of the Province of Bithynia. He wrote to the Emperor Trajan in about AD 112 (about seventeen years after the Apostle John's death). He sought guidance on how to deal with the sect of Christians. Pliny stated that the Christians assembled together regularly on a certain day "to sing responsively a certain hymn to Christ as if to a god". (Translation from Bruce M. Metzger, op. cit.)

Tacitus

Tacitus (c. AD 55-117) was a Roman historian. He wrote his *Annals*, covering the period AD14-68, in AD 115 (three years after Pliny's letter, about twenty years after the Apostle John's death). He stated:

Hence to suppress the rumour [that Nero was himself responsible for the fire which caused widespread destruction in Rome in AD 64] he falsely charged with the guilt, and punished with the most exquisite tortures, the persons commonly called Christians, who were hated for their enormities. Christus, the founder of the name, was put to death by Pontius Pilate, Procurator of Judea in the reign of Tiberius; but the pernicious superstition, repressed for a time, broke out again, not only through Judea, where the mischief originated, but through the city of Rome also.[5]

Suetonius

Suetonius (c. AD 70-130) served as secretary to the Emperor Hadrian, and wrote *The Lives of the Twelve Caesars* in about AD 120. In the section on Nero, he states that "the Emperor inflicted punishments on the Christians, a sect that professes a new and mischievous superstition". In the section on Claudius, he refers to the expulsion from Rome of the Jews, "who had been continually stirring up trouble under the influence of Chrestus".[6]

Lucian of Samosata

Lucian of Samosata (c. AD 125-180) was a Greek satirist. Writing in AD 170, he states:

> The Christians, you know, worship a man to this day - the distinguished personage who introduced their novel rights, and was crucified on that account…You see, these misguided creatures start with the general conviction that they are immortal for all time, which explains the contempt of death and voluntary self-devotion which are so common among them; and then it was impressed on them by their original lawgiver that they are all brothers, from the moment they are converted, and deny the gods of Greece, and worship the crucified sage, and live after his laws. All this they take quite on faith, with the result that they despise all worldly goods alike, regarding them merely as common property.[7]

Professor F.F. Bruce states: "Some writers may toy with the fancy of a 'Christ-myth', but they do not do so on the ground of historical evidence. The historicity of Christ is as axiomatic for an unbiased historian as the historicity of Julius Caesar. It is not historians who propagate the 'Christ-myth' theories."[8]

Bart D. Ehrman, who writes from a very different perspective - describing himself as "an agnostic with atheistic leanings…" - reaches a comparable conclusion. He examines the evidence in his book, *Did Jesus Exist?* and states his conclusion pithily: "Jesus did exist, whether we like it or not".[9]

Are the Gospel authors trustworthy?

The sacred authors, in writing the four Gospels, selected certain of the many elements which had been handed on, either orally or already in written form; others they synthesised or explained with an eye to the situation of the churches, the while sustaining the form of preaching, but always in such a fashion that they have told us the honest truth about Jesus.

(Dei Verbum)[10]

Evidence that Jesus existed only takes you so far. It is interesting and reassuring to find this (non-Christian) evidence, but that is far short of sufficient. We need detail. What did Jesus say? What did he do? That information is set out in the New Testament. But is it an accurate record of events?

There are a number of convincing reasons to believe that the record we have in the New Testament matches what was taught and written by contemporaries of Jesus, and that such teaching and writing recorded accurately widely observed events. The first reason is the character and knowledge of the authors.

Who are the authors?

The four Gospels bear the names of four contemporaries of Jesus - Matthew, Mark, Luke and John. If they were the authors, they were certainly in a position to make an accurate record.

- Matthew, also known as Levi, was a tax collector, and became an apostle as described in *Luke* 5:27, 28. His Gospel is particularly directed to a Jewish audience, with an emphasis on the role of Jesus as the long-expected Messiah, and the fulfilment of Old Testament prophesy.

- Mark, known as John Mark, was a companion of Peter. This Gospel refers often to Peter or to incidents involving Peter, and in such a way as to support the tradition that Mark based his Gospel on Peter's teaching. The Gospel is directed to a gentile, probably Roman, audience. It is generally accepted that this was the first of the four Gospels to be written.

- Luke, known as Paul's "beloved physician", travelled with Paul and is the author of Acts as well as this Gospel. Luke's Gospel is particularly directed to cultured Greeks and Romans. It uses the same overall design as Mark, but shares with Matthew additional material, particularly sayings of Jesus. This additional material may well derive from a separate collection (or perhaps several collections) of Jesus's sayings (often referred to as "Q"), in existence before Matthew or Luke wrote their Gospels.

* John, one of the earliest Apostles, was the brother of James and son of Zebedee. His Gospel is thought to be the last to have been written. John makes a particular feature of including extended comments by Jesus on particular themes.

Papias and Irenaeus

The tradition of the Church is that these four individuals are the authors, and we have two early pieces of evidence in support. The first comes from Papias (c. AD 70-163) and the second from Irenaeus (AD 130-202).

Papias was bishop of Hierapolis and was informed by disciples of the Apostles (and perhaps by the Apostle John himself). He stated that Mark recorded Peter's eyewitness observations, and "wrote accurately all that he remembered, not indeed, in order, of the things said or done by the Lord". His quote is preserved in the fourth century work by Eusebius, *Ecclesiastical History*.[11]

Irenaeus was bishop of Lyons in about AD 178. He knew St Polycarp (c. AD 69-155) who was a disciple of the Apostle John. Irenaeus wrote in about AD 180, and stated:

"Matthew published his own gospel among the Hebrews in their tongue, when Peter and Paul were preaching the gospel in Rome and founding the Church there. After their departure, Mark, the disciple and interpreter of Peter, himself handed down to us in writing the substance of Peter's preaching. Luke, the follower of Paul, set down in a book the gospel preached by his teacher. Then John, the disciple of the Lord, who also leaned on his breast, himself produced his Gospel while he was living at Ephesus in Asia."[12]

The Gospels are not signed, and the author's original material probably passed through several editions and was revised and updated. For example, in the case of John, the last few verses (which correct the erroneous belief that John would remain alive until the Second Coming) may well have been added immediately after John's death. Overall, it is reasonable to accept the long held Church tradition that substantially the material in the Gospels reflects the memory, knowledge, intention and work of the four named authors.

Invitations to verification

Anyone putting forward a minority view, a novel view, an unpopular view, appreciates the need to avoid "spoiling the ship for a hap' worth of tar". In other words, prejudicing acceptance of a fundamental truth of faith and philosophy by careless or wilful factual error. This was particularly important in relation to the Gospels, given the presence of so many eyewitnesses of the events re-told.

Caution might lead a political operator to a deliberate vagueness on verifiable detail; but that is not the case here.

Instead, again and again, specific names or places are cited.

- The centurion of great faith who comes to Capernaum to request healing for his servant, and is widely known as a benefactor of the Jews (*Mt* 7:5-8).

- The exorcism of the man in the synagogue in Capernaum on the Sabbath (*Mk* 1:21-27).

- The reference to Simon, whose house was in Bethany, who had suffered from a skin disease (*Mt* 26:6).

- The references to Joseph of Arimathea, a member of the Sanhedrin, presumably living in Jerusalem, who buried Jesus in his own tomb (*Lk* 23:50-53).

- The reference to Cleopas, who walked to Emmaus with another disciple, and saw and was instructed by Jesus after the Resurrection (*Lk* 24:18).

And many, many more. In each case, a name or a place, attached to a memorable event. Very easy to check, in these small towns and villages, where everyone knows everyone else, and their business. Did it happen at all? Did it happen like that? Impossible to include inaccurate detail.

Affirmations of accuracy and shared experience

The Gospels include many statements affirming expressly their accuracy, and appealing to knowledge of the events shared by author and audience.

- Luke's Prologue:

  "Seeing that many others have undertaken to draw up accounts of the events that have reached their fulfilment among us, as these were handed down to us by those who from the outset were eyewitnesses and ministers of the word, I in my turn, after carefully going over the whole story from the beginning, have decided to write an ordered account for you, Theophilus, so that Your Excellency may learn how well founded the teaching is that you received."

- Acts: "Jesus the Nazarene was a man commended to you by God by the miracles and portents and signs that God worked through him when he was among you, as you know." (*Ac* 2:22)

- John: "This is the evidence of one who saw it - true evidence, and he knows that what he says is true - and he gives it so that you may believe as well." (*Jn* 19:35)

- Peter: "When we told you about the power and the coming of our Lord Jesus Christ, we were not slavishly repeating cleverly invented myths; no, we had seen his majesty with our own eyes" (*2 P* 1:16).

How were the Gospels compiled?

A consideration of the actual state of the evidence will lead one to the conclusion that there was no large-scale introduction of extraneous material into the Gospels.

(Bruce M. Metzger)[13]

Following the Resurrection, Ascension and Pentecost, the Apostles preached their message of salvation with vigour and success. The message quickly attracted followers, who themselves relayed the faith. The Apostles themselves were present to teach, preach, correct and amplify the message for some time. Many survived into the 60s and 70s AD, and John to about AD 95.

The preaching and teaching was conducted in a society which depended upon and particularly valued accurate memory, accurate oral repetition. The rabbis taught that a good disciple is like a well-built cistern - he does not let fall one drop of his master's teaching.

Prompt oral repetition

There was no interlude between the events and their oral repetition, and little gap between the events and their written record. The oral repetition started at Pentecost - about seven weeks after the crucifixion. Elements were put into writing early - in the period AD 40-80. This was within the lifetime of a number of the Apostles; within the lifetime of many who had learnt from the Apostles; and of many who were eyewitnesses to the events taught orally and then recorded in the Gospels.

Written compilations

The earliest written records were probably short collections of the sayings of Jesus - grouped round separate themes. These may have been circulating by about AD 40-50. The Gospels (and Acts and the Letters) followed - and were completed relatively early. While scholars debate the most likely dates for the first and revised or edited versions of the Gospels, the following look reasonable estimates for the written Gospels:

- Mark, by about AD 64;
- Matthew and Luke before AD 70;
- John somewhat later, about AD 80.

That dating is based on both internal evidence - important matters which are, or are not, included, and on statements by early commentators.

- Mark: Clement of Alexandria (c. AD 150-215), who travelled extensively, studied Christianity in Alexandria and was ordained by Pope Julian, states that Mark wrote towards the end of Peter's life, and Irenaeus (c. AD 130-202) says he wrote shortly after Peter's death. Peter's death occurred in Rome in AD 64.

- Matthew and Luke: Their style and order suggest they wrote after Mark. However, neither refer to the destruction of Jerusalem (in AD 70). This was such a dramatic event, and one so apt for inclusion in a Gospel (since it both fulfilled prophesy and provided a terrible warning for those who failed to heed - indeed persecuted - Jesus and the Church) that a date before AD 70 looks appropriate. This fits in with the statement from Irenaeus, that Matthew's Gospel was written when Peter and Paul were preaching in Rome, which would suggest a date in the 60s. There is also the fact that Luke wrote his Gospel before he wrote Acts, so again a date before AD 70 is suggested.

- John: By about AD 80. Irenaeus states: "Last of all John, too, the disciple of the Lord who leant against his breast, himself brought out a Gospel when he was in Ephesus". John died as a very old man in AD 95.

- The Letters also have early dates. St Paul wrote his letters to the Thessalonians at some time between AD 50 and 52. His remaining letters followed over the next ten or so years. The letters therefore show that only twenty to thirty years after the crucifixion Christian communities were practising their faith in many different cities outside Judaea, and a developed understanding of the faith already existed.

- Acts: This contains a long section on the martyrdom of Stephen (somewhere around AD 32-33). There is, however, no mention of other, later, more significant events - the martyrdom of James (AD 62), Peter's trial (AD 64) and the destruction of Jerusalem (AD 70). All this suggests a date for Acts well before AD 70.

Have the Gospels been passed down to us accurately?

The number of manuscripts of the New Testament, of early translations from it, and of quotations from it in the oldest writers of the Church, is so large that it is practically certain that the true reading of every doubtful passage is preserved in some one or other of these ancient authorities. This can be said of no other ancient book in the world.

(Sir Frederic Kenyon)[14]

We do not have a piece of papyrus bearing Mark's signature (or Mathew's, Luke's or John's). We have, nevertheless, five grounds for reassurance that the "Gospels" we are reading are substantially the Gospels as originally written.

The early date of our surviving manuscripts

The John Rylands manuscript contains parts of St John's Gospel, and is dated (on the basis of the style of script) to somewhere between AD 100-150. The Bodmer Papyrus II contains most of John's Gospel and is dated around AD 200. The Chester Beatty Papyri contain major portions of the New Testament and are dated in the 200s.The Codex Vaticanus contains virtually the whole Bible and is dated

Page from the Codex Sinaiticus, Greek, (4th century AD).

AD 325-350. The Codex Sinaiticus contains almost all the New Testament and half the Old Testament and is dated AD 350. In every case the wording is in substance consistent with our modern Bible.

Professor F.F. Bruce notes that: "The evidence for our New Testament writings is ever so much greater than the evidence for many writings of classical authors, the authenticity of which no one dreams of questioning."[15]

The high number of surviving manuscripts

The position is vividly summarised by Josh McDowell in *The New Evidence That Demands a Verdict*:

> "There are now more than 5,686 known Greek manuscripts of the New Testament. Add over 10,000 Latin Vulgate and at least 9,300 other early versions (MSS), and we have close to, if not more than, 25,000 manuscript copies of portions of the New Testament in existence today. No other document of antiquity even begins to approach such numbers and attestation.
>
> In comparison, Homer's Iliad is second, with only 643 manuscripts that still survive."[16]

Consistency of content across different manuscripts

Our surviving manuscripts say, in all essentials, the same thing. This gives confidence on two levels. First, that scribes copied accurately over many eras and places;

second, that what we read reflects the earliest writing. There are, of course, spelling mistakes, different orders of words, duplications. But the fundamentals are consistent.

Lee Strobel sums up the position in a telling exchange with Dr Bruce M. Metzger, quoted in *The Case for Christ*:

> "How many doctrines of the Church are in jeopardy because of variants?" [ie variations between manuscripts]
>
> "I don't know of any doctrine that is in jeopardy."

The geographic spread of surviving manuscripts

The surviving manuscripts come from different, widely separated places, very different centres of study in the ancient world, with very different cultures - yet they say the same thing. This balances the "audit sample". It gives confidence that, across different cities, cultures, languages and eras, the same facts were being relayed.

External sources which quote the Gospels

Material in the Gospels is repeated or referred to in other early work from the era of the Apostolic Fathers (AD 90-160). Reading these other works provides a separate, corroborative source - of material separately prepared and copied, from an early date, which refers to much of the material in the Gospels and in substantially similar terms to the Gospels.

Does archeology support the Gospels?

Had the results of excavation in Israel turned out quite differently, one might want to argue that the testimony of the stones and artefacts called into question significant portions of the Evangelists' accounts. But that is not at all the impression one gets when one surveys a broad swathe of study of the relevant sites. Indeed, the results remain quite confirming of the Gospels' historical verisimilitude.

(Craig L. Blomberg)[17]

There is a consistency between information in the Gospels and information on the same matters from archaeological sources. That is important, not merely to confirm specific detail, but to give confidence that the author was of an accurate cast of mind, and his comments have come down to us accurately. Josh McDowell and Bill Wilson produce an impressive list of archaeological verification in *He Walked Among Us*. Here are a few examples.

People and places

Pontius Pilate: In 1961, excavations in Caesarea unearthed an inscription in Latin "Pontius Pilate, Prefect of Judaea, has presented the Tiberium to the Caesareans". This therefore provides external confirmation of Pilate's name and office.

Nazareth: In 1962, excavations in Caesaria unearthed two fragments of an inscription referring to Nazareth, in the context of the period following the destruction of the Temple in AD 70. This provided clear evidence of the existence of the village in New Testament times - something which had been doubted because of a lack of references to it outside the Gospels. It seems Nazareth was an insignificant and unimportant village - perhaps the background to Nathaniel's comment: "From Nazareth? Can anything good come from that place?" (*Jn* 1:46)

The texture of life

Stone water pots: The first miracle, at the marriage feast in Cana, is very well known. The Bible refers to six water pots, holding twenty or thirty gallons each. Some have suggested that such pots were rare, luxury items (and therefore unlikely to be present at the Cana marriage). Excavations by Professor Nahman Avigad showed otherwise. He wrote: "The discovery of stone vessels became a routine matter in our work, for whenever we approached a stratum of the Second Temple period, and a building that was burnt during the destruction of the city in AD 70 began revealing itself, they invariably made their appearance as well."

Crucifixion: The Gospels report the use of nails to fasten the victim to the cross, and the breaking of the legs of the criminals executed with Jesus. Scepticism has been expressed that such practices in fact took place. In 1968 four cave tombs were excavated near Jerusalem. Tomb One, dating back to the first century AD, included the skeleton of an adult male. The report from the Department of Anatomy of the Hebrew Medical School stated: "Both the heel bones were found transfixed by a large iron nail. The shins were found intentionally broken. Death caused by crucifixion".

Official titles

Luke has been found to be remarkably accurate in his use of official titles. For example:

- Luke refers to Sergius Paulus as "Proconsul" of Cyprus, which reflected the status of the island as a senatorial province (not an imperial province, governed by an imperial legate). The change in status occurred in 22 BC.

- Luke refers to the ruler of Malta as "the first man of the island". Greek and Latin inscriptions show this unusual title was indeed the correct title at the time of the events recorded.

Professor F.F. Bruce puts it well in *The New Testament Documents: Are They Reliable?*:

> Now, all these evidences of accuracy are not accidental. A man whose accuracy can be demonstrated in matters where we are able to test it is likely to be accurate even where the means for testing him are not available. Accuracy is a habit of mind, and we know from happy (or unhappy) experience that some people are habitually accurate just as others can be depended upon to be inaccurate. Luke's record entitles him to be regarded as a writer of habitual accuracy.

What does Truth look like?

I will confess against myself mine own unrighteousness. To thee, O Lord, will I acknowledge my weakness. Oftentimes it is but a little thing that causeth me to be dejected and troubled. I resolve to meet evil courageously, but when even a small temptation cometh, I am in sore straights...behold, therefore, O Lord, my low estate and my frailty, which are in every way known to Thee. Have mercy upon me, and deliver me out of the mire, that I may sink not therein, nor be utterly cast down forever.

(Thomas à Kempis)[18]

We are flawed creatures, all of us. Any serious self-examination is painful. How we tend to avoid it, make light of or excuse faults; denominate deep seated defects of character as mere occasional failings. And just as we are reluctant to see the raw truth about ourselves, so we also seek the comfort of illusions about our world. We are ever inclined to give credit to some new paradigm, where 2+2=5.

In our more sensible moments, we trust those who have the courage and honesty to require us to confront our true selves, and who tell of a world which reflects our own experience - a patched thing, good and bad.

One of the impressive features of the Gospels is their inclusion of "adverse" material. The disciples behave badly on occasion; we are warned that the Christian life will be a hard one; sometimes Jesus appears to lack the anticipated qualities of a Messiah. There is even the point that the first witnesses to the Resurrection are recorded as women - culturally at that time not the best form of evidence.

The disciples fall short

- Lack of faith: When a squall of wind came down on the lake the boat started shipping water and they found themselves in danger. So they went to rouse him saying, "Master! Master! We are lost!" Then he woke up and rebuked the wind and the rough water; and they subsided and it was calm again. He said to them, "Where is your faith?" (*Lk* 8:23-25)

- Pride: An argument started between them about which of them was the greatest. Jesus knew what thoughts were going through their minds, and he took a little child whom he set by his side and then he said to them, "Anyone who welcomes this little child in my name welcomes me; and anyone who welcomes me, welcomes the one who sent me. The least among you all is the one who is the greatest."(*Lk* 9:47-48)

- Desertion: Then they came forward, seized Jesus and arrested him. Then all the disciples deserted him and ran away. (*Mt* 26:56)

- Disbelief: And they [the women] returned from the tomb and told all this to the Eleven and to all the others, but this story of theirs seemed pure nonsense, and they did not believe them. (*Lk* 24:9-11)

The hardship and demands of Christian life

- Take up the cross: He called the people and his disciples to him and said, "If anyone wants to be a follower of mine, let him renounce himself and take up his cross and follow me. Anyone who wants to save his life will lose it; but anyone who loses his life for my sake, and for the sake of the Gospel, will save it." (*Mk* 8:34-35)

- Exacting moral standards: You have heard how it was said, "You shall not commit adultery." But I say this to you, if a man looks at a woman lustfully, he has already committed adultery with her in his heart. If your right eye should be your downfall, tear it out and throw it away; for it will do you less harm to lose one part of yourself than to have your whole body thrown into hell. (*Mt* 5:27-29)

- Hard choices: Enter by the narrow gate, since the road that leads to destruction is wide and spacious, and many take it; but it is a narrow gate and a hard road that leads to life, and only a few find it. (*Mt* 7:13, 14)

Is this the Messiah?

- Baptism: Then Jesus appeared: he came from Galilee to the Jordan to be baptised by John. John tried to dissuade him, with the words, "It is I who need Baptism from you, and yet you come to me!" But Jesus replied, "Leave it like this for the time being; it is fitting that we should, in this way, do all that uprightness demands". (*Mt* 3:13-15)

- Few miracles in Nazareth: Leaving that district, he went to his home town, and his disciples accompanied him… And they would not accept him.

  And Jesus said to them, "A prophet is despised only in his own country, among his own relations and in his own house"; and he could work no miracle there, except that he cured a few sick people by laying his hands on them. He was amazed at their lack of faith. (*Mk* 6:1, 4-6)

- Limits to knowledge on earth: Sky and earth will pass away, but my words will never pass away. But as for that day and hour [the Second Coming], nobody knows it, neither the angels of heaven, nor the Son, no one but the Father alone. (*Mt* 24:35-36)

- Desperation on the cross: When the sixth hour came there was darkness over the whole land until the ninth hour. Jesus cried out in a loud voice, "Eloi, Eloi, lama sabachhtani?" which means, "My God, my God, why have you forsaken me?" (*Mk* 15:33-34)

It is important to add a note in relation to the cry of desperation on the cross, which can readily be misunderstood. Jesus's words are a quotation from Psalm 22. The psalm begins with this cry of desperation, from a persecuted innocent. It moves on through an appeal to God, an undertaking to praise God and to a conviction that "The whole wide world will remember and return to Yahweh, all the families of nations bow down before him." So, in the midst of terrible suffering, Jesus uses the words of a psalm which affirms the existence of, reverence for, help from and ultimate triumph of, God.

The inclusion of all this apparently adverse material in the Gospels is convincing, because it must have been tough to tell people about, to write, to form the basis of missionary work in an already unsympathetic (to put it mildly) world. How tempting to trim; but they did not. The authors felt an obligation to tell the exact truth; and had the confidence to know that this truth was powerful - even with these human weaknesses and adversities displayed.

The cultural background

Overall, you should not only know your audience, but also feel their feelings, needs and hopes... But most of all these occasions are about gauging the mood of, listening to, responding to and trying to achieve a real connection with the audience.

(Richard Hall)[19]

Did Jesus know that he was God? Did he say so?
The short answers are "Yes" and "Yes". But to appreciate why Jesus chose to use particular forms of self-description, and to make his statements to particular audiences on particular occasions, one needs some understanding of the Jewish religious culture of his time.

A reverential culture; a messianic expectation

The culture of the Jews of Jesus's day was strongly monotheistic and strongly reverential. There was no general recognition of the concept of the Trinity. It was also strongly expectant of the coming of the "Messiah".

The title "Messiah" is a Hebrew word meaning "anointed", which in Greek is "Christos" and in English "Christ". In Jesus's time, the Messianic expectation among the Jews (but not among the Samaritans) was for a warrior king, who would "redeem" Israel by freeing the nation from Rome.

This widespread expectation gave rise to a problem. Jesus's message was indeed that he was the Messiah; through him, redemption has come to all mankind.

Sins could now be forgiven, all could reach heaven after death. But this redemption was personal, individual and achieved through cleansing one's own heart. It required sacrifice of self; it required love of God and love of neighbour. Ritualistic practice had a place, but a subordinate one.

The popular expectation of the time, that the Messiah would be a warrior king, who would achieve a new political and social world order through military success, was wholly misconceived.

The risk for Jesus was that a plain, public statement that he was the Messiah, that he was God, would close, not open, men's minds. Instead of the crucial need to listen, to understand, to examine one's own conscience against the standards of love for God and neighbour, to change one's heart, the words would instead prompt emotion, violence, military ambition, an attempt at political revolution.

That is why Jesus "gave the disciples strict orders not to say to anyone that he was the Christ" (*Mt* 16:20). That is why he used the terminology he did, and in the circumstances he did.

How did Jesus describe himself?

"Who is he?" (Mk 8:27-30). The answers of the "people" in the time of Jesus, as reported in the Gospels, reflect the attempt to find, in the arsenal of the known and nameable, categories in which to describe the figure of Jesus.

(Cardinal Ratzinger, later Pope Benedict XVI)[20]

The hardest part of thinking is to grasp something new. We always tend to look back, to explain what we see now by what we already know, what we have seen before. We try to place the new wine into old skins. It doesn't work; but it takes time and painful experience for most of us to admit it, and to be open to the new.

Jesus was clear about his nature and powers; but it was some time before even the Apostles grasped the consequences, understood the inevitable result.

Pre-existence

In all truth I tell you,
Before Abraham ever was,
I am. *(Jn 8:58)*

He said to them, "I watched Satan fall
like lightning from heaven." *(Lk 10:18)*

Now, Father, glorify me
With that glory I had with you
Before ever the world existed. (*Jn* 17:5)

The relationship of the Father and Jesus

Philip said, "Lord, show us the Father and then we shall be satisfied". Jesus said to him, "Have I been with you all this time, Philip, and you still do not know me? Anyone who has seen me has seen the Father, so how can you say, 'Show us the Father?' Do you not believe that I am in the Father and the Father is in me?" (*Jn* 14:8-10)

Everything has been entrusted to me by my Father; and no one knows the Son except the Father, just as no one knows the Father except the Son and those to whom the Son chooses to reveal him. (*Mt* 11:27)

The power of Jesus to judge, to forgive sins, to give eternal life

For the Father judges no one;
He has entrusted all judgement to the Son,
So that all may honour the Son
As they honour the Father. (*Jn* 5:22-23)

It is not anyone who says to me, "Lord, Lord", who will enter the kingdom of heaven, but the person who does the will of my Father in heaven. When the day comes, many will say to me, "Lord, Lord, did we not prophesy in your name, drive out demons in your name, work many miracles in your name?" Then I shall tell them to their faces: "I have never known you; away from me all evil doers!" (*Mt* 7:21-23)

…they stripped the roof over the place where Jesus was; and when they had made an opening, they lowered the stretcher on which the paralytic lay. Seeing their faith, Jesus said to the paralytic, "My child, your sins are forgiven". (*Mk* 2:4-5)

The Jews gathered round him and said, "How much longer are you going to keep us in suspense? If you are the Christ, tell us openly." Jesus replied: "I have told you, but you do not believe.
The works I do in my Father's name are my witness;
but you do not believe,
because you are no sheep of mine.
The sheep that belong to me listen to my voice;
I know them and they follow me.
I give them eternal life;
they will never be lost
and no one will ever steal them from my hand.
The Father, for what he has given me,
is greater than anyone,
And no one can steal anything from the Father's hand.
The Father and I are one." (*Jn* 10:24-30)

Jesus has the power to lay down, and take up, his life

The Father loves me,
because I lay down my life
in order to take it up again.
No one takes it from me;
I lay it down of my own free will,
as I have power to lay it down,
so I have power to take it up again
and this is the command I have received from my Father.
(*Jn* 10:17, 18)

Jesus uses the "I AM" name of God

Moses then said to God, "Look, if I go to the Israelites and say to them, 'The God of your ancestors has sent me to you,' and they say to me, 'What is his name?' What am I to tell them?" God said to Moses, "I AM he who is". And he said, "this is what you are to say to the Israelites, 'I AM has sent me to you'." (*Ex* 3:13, 14)

I AM the light of the world;
anyone who follows me will not be walking in the dark but will have the light of life. (*Jn* 8:12)

Yes, if you do not believe that I AM he,
You will die in your sins. (*Jn* 8:24)

I AM the Resurrection. Anyone who believes in me, even though that person dies, will live, and whoever lives and believes in me will never die. *(Jn 11:2)*

Contemporary Jewish religious authorities understood Jesus's claim as one to divinity

Jesus said, "Get up, pick up your sleeping mat and walk around."

The man was cured at once, and he picked up his mat and started to walk around. Now that day happened to be the Sabbath...it was because he did things like this on the Sabbath that the Jews began to harass Jesus. His answer to them was, "My Father still goes on working, and I am at work too." But this only made the Jews even more intent on killing him, because not only was he breaking the Sabbath, but he spoke of God as his own Father and so made himself God's equal. *(Jn 5:8-10; 16-18)*

Jesus replied:

"The Father and I are one." The Jews fetched stones to stone him, so Jesus said to them, "I have shown you many good works from my Father, for which of these are you stoning me?" The Jews answered him,

"We are stoning you, not for doing a good work, but for blasphemy; though you are only a man, you claim to be God". *(Jn 10:25, 30, 31-33)*

The high priest put a second question to him saying, "Are you the Christ, the Son of the Blessed One?" "I am", said Jesus, "and you will see the Son of man seated at the right hand of the Power and coming with the clouds of heaven". The high priest tore his robes and said, "What need of witnesses have we now? You heard the blasphemy. What is your finding?" Their verdict was unanimous; he deserved to die. (*Mk* 14:61-64.)

Jesus stated that he was the long awaited Messiah

- The condemnation at his trial followed Jesus's own citation, in relation to himself, of the Old Testament prophesy of Daniel relating to the Messiah:

I was gazing into the visions of the night, when I saw, coming on the clouds of heaven, as it were a son of man. on him was conferred rule,
Honour and kingship,
And all peoples, nations and languages
became his servants.
His rule is an everlasting rule
Which will never pass away
And his kingship will never come to an end.
(*Dn* 7:13, 14)

- Now John had heard in prison what Christ was doing and he sent his disciples to ask him, "Are you the one who is to come, or are we to expect someone else?"

Jesus answered, "Go back and tell John what you hear and see; the blind see again, and the lame walk, those suffering from virulent skin diseases are cleansed, and the deaf hear, the dead are raised to life and the good news is proclaimed to the poor; and blessed is anyone who does not find me a cause for falling." (*Mt* 11:2-6)

- This deliberately echoes the prophecy in Isaiah about the coming of the Messiah:

  Then the eyes of the blind will be opened
  the ears of the deaf unsealed,
  then the lame will leap like a deer
  and the tongue of the dumb sing for joy; (*Is* 35:5, 6)

- The [Samaritan] woman said to him, "I know that Messiah - that is, Christ - is coming; and when he comes he will explain everything."

- Jesus said, "That is who I AM, I who speak to you". (*Jn* 4:25-26)

- "But you," he said, "Who do you say I AM?" Then Simon Peter spoke up and said, "You are the Christ, the son of the living God". Jesus replied, "Simon son of Jonah, you are a blessed man! Because it was no human agency that revealed this to you but my Father in heaven". (*Mt* 16:15-17)

- "You foolish men! So slow to believe all that the prophets have said! Was it not necessary that the Christ should suffer before entering into his glory?" Then, starting with Moses and going through all the prophets, he explained to them the passages throughout the scriptures that were about himself. (*Lk* 24:25-27)

Understanding Jesus through his actions

I have always thought the actions of men the best interpreters of their thoughts.

(John Locke)[21]

There are two key issues here: the miracles, and the extraordinary wisdom and love displayed in daily life by Jesus.

The miracles

Jesus performs miracles of three different types:

- Nature miracles, where he alters the normal pattern of nature - for example calming the waves on the Lake of Galilee (*Lk* 8:22-25) and the feeding of the five thousand (*Lk* 9:12-17).

- Healing miracles, where he cures the sick and afflicted (and raises the dead), such as the cure of the man with the withered hand in the synagogue (*Mt* 12:9-13); the cure of the centurion's servant (*Lk* 7:3-10); and the raising of Lazarus (*Jn* 11:1), the widow of Nain's son (*Lk* 7:11) and Jairus's daughter (*Mk* 5:21).

- Knowledge miracles, where he foretells the future, such as his crucifixion (*Mt* 26:1-2) or shows knowledge of events he has not seen, such as Nathaniel seated under a fig tree before Philip called him (*Jn* 1:48).

It is unrealistic to argue that these events "did not happen"- that they were invented. The early date of the Gospels, the local sites, the large number of witnesses and the controversy over Jesus (and Christianity) make it untenable to claim that "something" did not happen.

Nor is it feasible to claim that the healings were psychosomatic and the natural miracles fortuitous accidents of nature. The detailed descriptions take many of these events outside those possibilities - both as to the nature of the cure or event (the cure of blindness; deafness; a withered hand; skin diseases; fever; raising those pronounced dead; the feeding of the five thousand), and the odds against such a number of extraordinary events all following the specific intervention of Jesus.

Daily life

The record of the daily round is, in a different, less dramatic way, also profoundly moving and convincing. Again and again, the response, parable or answer given by Jesus is at first sight surprising, on reflection deeply wise. Many of them have become embedded in our language. The action of the Good Samaritan, helping his enemy the Jew, when the victim's fellow Jews have passed by on the other side; the forgiveness, and welcome, to the humbled and repentant Prodigal Son; the warning to the workers in the vineyard who become discontented on seeing the generosity offered to latecomers; the response on taxes -

render unto Caesar what is Caesar's, to God what is God's; the reassurance against worry, with the marvellous comfort that Solomon in all his glory failed to compare with the beauty of flowers; the merciful reaction to the woman taken in adultery, and to the woman who was a sinner and brought ointment for Jesus at Simon the Pharisee's house. In both these two cases, a reminder to the upright: show love, judge not since you yourself are flawed.

Again and again we find ourselves in the presence of profound wisdom and love - but never sloppiness or sentimentality. There are real standards for us to follow, and real and terrible consequences for our failure (as for the rich man, Dives, who ignores the beggar Lazarus at his gate) (*Lk* 16:19). But again and again the refrain directs us to love of God and neighbour, to unselfishness.

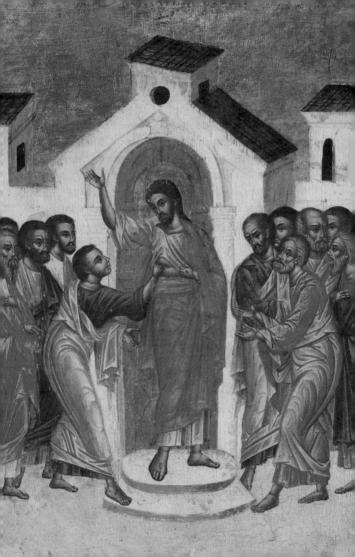

The Resurrection

For the blessed flesh and bones were left all alone without blood and moisture. The blessed body dried alone a long time, with wringing of the nails, weight of the head, and weight of the body. For I understood that for tenderness of the sweet hands and of the sweet feet, by the largeness, hardness, and grievousness of the nails, the wounds waxed wide and the body sagged by the weight hanging a long time, and the piercing and wringing of the head and binding of the crown all baked with dry blood with the sweet hair clinging and the dry flesh to the thorns, and the thorns to the dying flesh.

(Julian of Norwich)[22]

The Resurrection is the culmination of a sequence involving extreme mental and physical suffering and death. A clear understanding of that sequence is needed in order to think accurately about the Resurrection.

The agony in the garden

The sequence starts with Jesus praying in the Garden of Gethsemane. He is aware of what is to come. His mental agony is vividly described: "In his anguish he prayed even more earnestly, and his sweat fell to the ground like great drops of blood" (*Lk* 22:44).

The Jerusalem Bible translates this as a simile. Other translations treat it literally. Interestingly, it is possible to sweat blood, a condition known as Hematidrosis. In times of great anxiety, chemicals are released which break down the capillaries in the sweat glands. Sweat then released comes out tinged with blood. The condition also makes the skin for a time very sensitive and fragile.

The flogging

After the arrest come the trials, and then the flogging. Roman flogging often consisted of thirty nine lashes (but could be more) delivered with a whip. The whip had braided leather thongs, with metal balls and pieces of sharp bone attached. The metal balls caused deep bruising, which would break open with further blows. The bone would cause deep cuts. As the flogging continued, the lacerations would tear into underlying skeletal muscles; the spine might be exposed; ribbons of flesh would be stripped from the back.

Many people died in the course of, or after, such a beating. If you survived, you would be suffering from Hypovolemic shock. Blood pressure drops; the heart races; the kidneys stop producing urine; the sufferer feels faint and may collapse, and becomes very thirsty. This is, of course, consistent with the Gospel record of the soldiers needing to conscript Simon of Cyrene to carry the cross (*Lk* 23:26) and Jesus saying "I thirst" (*Jn* 19:28).

The crucifixion

First, sharp spikes, five to seven inches long, were driven through the wrists, to attach them to the crossbeam of the cross. The spikes crush the median nerve as they are pounded in. This is the largest nerve running into the hand. Then a spike was driven through the feet (probably the heel bones). The pain would be extreme.

The effect of hanging from the cross would be to dislocate both shoulders and stretch the arms about six inches. As Psalm 22 says "My bones are out of joint".

Once the victim is hanging vertically, breathing becomes very difficult. The victim must push himself upwards - causing great pain in the feet, and rubbing a flogged back against the cross. As the breathing slows, the carbon dioxide in the blood is dissolved as carbonic acid, the acidity of the blood increases and the heartbeat becomes irregular.

Death in crucifixion came from either asphyxiation or heart failure.

The practice of breaking legs was used to hasten death. Once the victim could no longer push himself upright, asphyxiation followed.

Sustained rapid heartbeat and heart failure leads to the collection of fluid in the membrane around the heart (pericardial effusion) and in the lungs (pleural effusion). This was the clear liquid that, with blood, flowed out of Jesus's side when pierced with a lance (*Jn* 19:34).

A gruesome subject. There are detailed descriptions in *The Case for Christ* by Lee Strobel and *Evidence That Demands a Verdict* by Josh McDowell. The detail is important, for two reasons. First, to understand the degree of suffering Jesus willingly underwent for our salvation. Second, to dispense with theories that Jesus did not die on the cross - he fainted or was drugged, and later recovered. The reality is that there can be no recovery from these injuries.

The burial

Jesus was then buried in a previously unused tomb owned by Joseph of Arimathea, a member of the Sanhedrin. The body would typically be washed and wrapped in a white linen shroud, probably with spices mixed with myrrh (an adhesive).

The tomb would be closed by removing the wedge in front of a large, disc-shaped rock in front of the tomb. The rock was then rolled down a sloping, grooved track, coming to rest in front of the entrance *(Mt* 27:60). It was then sealed with a Roman seal, and guarded by soldiers (*Mt* 27:64).

On the third day, first women, then two disciples came to the tomb and found the stone rolled away, the guard fled and the tomb empty. Over the next forty days, a large number of people - over five hundred - saw Jesus, he spoke to them, walked with them and ate with them. The Jewish authorities apparently spread the story that the disciples had stolen the body. So what happened?

Was the tomb empty?

Had the body really gone? Some sceptics have suggested that either no one knew where Jesus had been buried, or the women and disciples went to the wrong tomb - a new, open one which had never been used.

These theories do not work. Not only are the women recorded as having noted, at the time of the burial, the new tomb used by Joseph of Arimathea (*Lk* 23:55), but also if the body was available, in a tomb with a guard of soldiers organised by the Jewish authorities, then those authorities would have produced the body, to destroy the new Christian sect.

A real Resurrection

The absent body also means that comments that the Resurrection was merely a spiritual, intangible event (which would, of course, leave the dead body in its place in the tomb) are incorrect. If there had been a body in the tomb, the response from Jewish authorities would be decisive - Here is the Corpse!

Removal of the body

Sceptics who accept that the body had gone from the tomb suggest either that it was removed by the Jewish authorities or by the Apostles.

Neither suggestion survives consideration.

If the Jewish authorities removed the body, they would

have been able to produce it, destroying the rumour and belief in the Resurrection. They did not.

If the Apostles removed the body, it is unbelievable that they then spoke of the Resurrection, based their faith on it, endured lives of poverty and suffering for it, and were eventually martyred for it.

No death: the swoon

Another sceptics' theory is that of the "swoon": Jesus fainted on the cross, but revived in the tomb and escaped - hence accounting both for the empty tomb and the "Resurrection" appearances.

Again, a moment's consideration undermines the theory.

First, survival after the crucifixion (including the stab through the ribs) is not a credible possibility. Second, the soldiers would have had to be mistaken as to death - highly unlikely. Third, a terribly injured man would have had to free himself from the linen bindings mixed with adhesive; roll away the rock from the entrance (silently); evade the tomb guards; find fresh clothes and recover sufficiently to walk and talk, to eat, to teach (the road to Emmaus), to address groups of followers (and move through walls and appear and disappear); again, beyond credibility.

The third party, the double, hallucination

Another group of sceptical theories suggest that Jesus was removed (live or dead) from the tomb by a third party (previously and subsequently unidentified) and disappears - he goes to live in India or Egypt (if alive) or is reburied somewhere unknown (if dead). The resurrection appearances are explained either by a "body double" being seen, or by a widely shared hallucination or a vision produced by hypnosis.

The first element, removal of the body, faces the same problems as noted above - the difficulty of moving the rock and evading the guards with a dead or appallingly injured man.

The second part - the double - is even more incredible. A double would need the same scars as Jesus (remember doubting Thomas, who believed only when, at the invitation of Jesus, he saw and touched the wounds); would need deep biblical learning (the teaching on the road to Emmaus); and would have to be so similar as to be recognised by over five hundred people. And who made the arrangements? Jesus? He would thus show himself to be an extraordinary fraud (in which case why die an agonising death?) Or an "officious bystander", an independent third party (but how could he create the same wounds, learning, manner, appearance), and why?

The hallucination/hypnosis theories also fall apart
on detailed review.

Hallucination tends to act on certain types of people; over a long period; reflecting their own subconscious; and derived from anticipation. None of those factors are present in relation to the appearances of Jesus. Over five hundred different people, some as individuals some in small groups, some in larger gatherings (in one case five hundred people together - *1 Co* 15:6) witnessed the resurrected Christ - they would not all have the same type of psychological profile or share the same subconscious drives; most of them certainly did not anticipate Jesus's return (consider the reactions of the Apostles, and of Thomas, on first hearing news of Jesus's Resurrection).

Hypnosis is rather different, but equally flawed on investigation. The theory assumes that Jesus (in his lifetime) deliberately hypnotised the Apostles (and every single one of more than five hundred other witnesses). Incredible as a physical feat; even more incredible psychologically. Here was a man preaching on truth, forgiveness, judgement, heaven and hell, a man prepared to die for his beliefs - whom it is suggested plans the deliberate deceit of his followers - and history. Simply not believable.

Conclusion

The conclusion is that the reports in the Gospels, the reactions of the Apostles and the reactions of the very rapidly growing band of converts, were correct. Jesus died and rose again. His risen body was a physical one, he could talk, eat, move, and his appearance and voice were identifiable with his pre-crucifixion body - but also had some special features - ability to appear and disappear instantly, to pass through walls.

The conduct of the Apostles

But for footmen like you and me, let us never hope to meet an enemy, or boast that we could do better, when we hear of others who have been attacked. Let us not be fooled by thoughts of our own manhood. We would get the worst of it. Witness Peter, whom I mentioned before, he would swagger. Yes, he would. His conceited mind prompted him to say that he would do better for his Master than anyone. Yet who was so defeated and run down by villains as he?

(John Bunyan)[23]

The Apostles changed, changed fundamentally, and changed for good and all: that's the point. Prior to his post-Resurrection appearances, their record was a patchy one. Yes, they had decided to follow Jesus. That was an impressive step. But they remained prone to very human failings. Their understanding was slow ("Do you not understand this parable?" [the parable of the sower]: *Mk* 4:13); their faith was limited ("Have you still no faith?" when they panic in the storm on the Lake of Galilee: *Mk* 4:35-41); and fragile (Peter stepping out of the boat onto the sea of Galilee to walk to Jesus, then feeling the wind and sinking: *Mt* 14:22-33); they were ambitious

(James and John asking for the "best seats" in Heaven: *Mk* 10:35-38); competitive ("...on the road they had been arguing which of them was the greatest": *Mk* 9:34).

Above all, their weakness at the time of the crucifixion. They slept while Jesus endured the mental struggle in the Garden of Gethsemane; they fled when Jesus was arrested; only Peter and one other followed to the chief priest's house; and Peter famously denied Jesus three times before the cock crowed. Only one (John) is mentioned as being present at the crucifixion. Afterwards, the first reaction to the women's report of the empty tomb is scepticism. Even after Mary of Magdala's report that she has seen the risen Jesus, the Apostles stay together in a room with the doors closed (presumably locked) "for fear of the Jews" (*Jn* 20:19). Thomas famously doubts even the statement of the other Apostles that they have seen Jesus.

A transformation unto death

Then, all changes. After the Resurrection comes a period of Jesus's appearances and teaching; the Apostles grow in faith and understanding. A week after the Ascension, the Holy Spirit comes at Pentecost. The Apostles are, indeed, transformed. They preach and teach, work miracles, found a church and expand it across the Roman Empire. They undertake lives of extraordinary hardship, poverty and suffering as they travel on their missionary journeys. Jesus had warned them (*Mk* 12:9-13), and the warnings proved true. Finally, all of the disciples (or perhaps all save John) were martyred; they refused to recant to save themselves.

These transformed Apostles are the very people who knew Jesus; who knew all the people and places involved. One of them was present at the crucifixion, all knew people who had been there. They probably knew Joseph of Arimathea; they knew the women who first found the empty tomb; they knew Lazarus and Mary and Martha; they knew of Pilate, were likely to have seen him on formal, public occasions; knew, or knew of, the members of the Sanhedrin; knew Golgotha; knew Our Lady.

They knew what they had seen, what they were preaching about. They were confident to preach on events which happened in small towns and villages, where people could readily verify the factual details stated by the Apostles (and their followers); and to preach to audiences which included people who lived where the events had taken place, knew people who had been involved. They were confident that the factual background of what they said was true, and their hearers would recognise it.

The belief of the early Church

The devotional practices of the primitive Church, for which there is substantial evidence, clearly demonstrate that Jesus was worshipped as divine right from the beginning of the Christian movement.

(Dean L. Overman)[24]

The Church, from its earliest days, acted and spoke in a manner which demonstrated a belief that Jesus was divine, was one with God. This was not a late addition to its philosophy. It was established at a time when many (indeed most) eyewitnesses to the events recorded in the Gospels were alive. For example, Philippians (quoted below) was written sometime between about AD 56-62, and the extracts quoted are generally thought to represent hymns already used at that time in the early Church. Paul's first letter to the Corinthians (quoted below) was written in Ephesus in AD 56 or 57, and appears to pass on, word for word, teaching Paul himself received from Peter, James and John when he stayed with them in Jerusalem sometime around AD 36-38.

The Sabbath

Respect for the Sabbath - buttressed by many rules of conduct - was a cornerstone of Jewish religious practice and daily life. It reflected God's command, relayed by Moses, to rest and focus on God on one day in the week (although the particular day was not specified in God's command): *Ex* 20:8.

Yet followers of Christ felt empowered to replace the Saturday Sabbath with a Lord's Day on Sunday. The change demonstrates both the fundamental importance of the day of the Resurrection, and the "status" of Jesus - his commemoration justified overturning a tradition of centuries founded by Moses.

The title of "Kyrios" or "Lord"

The Jewish name for God was YHWH - Yahweh. Such was the reverence of the Jews for God's name that it was not spoken or written. Accordingly, when Jews referred to God they used the Hebrew word "Adonai", the Aramaic name "Mareh" or the Greek word "*Kyrios*", translated as "Lord" in English.

Paul, the ex Pharisee, uses "*Kyrios*" when referring to Yahweh. For example: "How blessed are those to whom the Lord [*Kyrios*] imputes no guilt" (*Rm* 4:8, quoting *Ps* 32:1-2).

Josephus notes that the Jews would not refer to the Roman Emperor as "*Kyrios*" - since that would have been to equate his title with God.

However, the early Church used the term "*Kyrios*" for Jesus, thus treating him in the same way as God. Peter, in

1 *Peter* 3:15 states: "Simply proclaim the Lord [*Kyrios*] Christ holy in your hearts, and always have your answer ready for people who ask you the reason for the hope that you have."

Paul writes in *Romans* 10:9: "…if you declare with your mouth that Jesus is Lord [*Kyrios*] and if you believe with your heart that God raised him from the dead, then you will be saved."

Peter, in his great Pentecost speech, refers to Jesus as "*Kyrios*".

A related point is the use of the "MARANATHA" invocation in relation to Jesus. The Aramaic phrase (the language used by Jesus and the early Church in Jerusalem) means "Lord, Come" or "The Lord is coming" or "Our Lord, Come". It is used in relation to Jesus in ritual and prayer. Paul uses it (*1 Co* 16:22); it is used in *Revelation* (Epilogue) and in the *Didache* (the guidance for Christian prayer and ritual, written between AD 65 and 85). The phrase presupposes that Jesus is alive; is able to come among his followers in some way, is properly addressed as "Lord". Jesus is treated wholly differently from an angel or a prophet. Abraham, Moses, David are never spoken of in this way.

Recognition that Jesus shares the nature and powers of God

The early Church was clear in recognising that Jesus *shared* the nature and powers of God the Father which are identified in the Old Testament. Comparison of Old and New Testament readings makes this clear.

- Whom to call holy, whom to fear:

  Yahweh Sabaoth is the one you will proclaim holy, him you will dread, him you will fear. (*Is* 8:13)

  No one can hurt you if you are determined to do only what is right; and blessed are you if you have to suffer for being upright. Have no dread of them; have no fear. Simply proclaim the Lord Christ holy in your hearts, and always have your answer ready for people who ask you the reason for the hope that you have. (*1 P* 3:15)

- Salvation:

  All who call on the name of Yahweh will be saved. (*Jl* 3:5)

  "…if you declare with your mouth that Jesus is Lord, and if you believe with your heart that God raised him from the dead, then you will be saved. It is by believing with the heart that you are justified, and by making the declaration with your lips that you are saved." (*Rm* 10:9-13)

- Unique and supreme:

    Thus says Yahweh:
    Turn to me and you will be saved,
    For I am God, and there is no other,
    By my own self I swear it;
    All shall bend the knee to me. (*Is* 45:14, 22-23)

    And for this God raised him high,
    And gave him the name
    Which is above all other names;
    So that all beings
    In the heavens, on earth and in the underworld,
    Should bend the knee at the name of Jesus. (*Ph* 2:9, 10)

- Creator:

    In the beginning God created heaven and earth...
    God said "Let the earth produce every kind of living
    creature..." (*Gn* 1:1, 24)

    "Make your own the mind of Christ Jesus:
    Who, being in the form of God
    Did not count equality with God
    Something to be grasped.
    But he emptied himself,
    Taking the form of a slave,
    Becoming as human beings are... (*Ph* 2:1-9)

"He is the image of the unseen God,
The first-born of all creation,
For in him were created all things
In heaven and on earth;
everything visible and everything invisible,
He exists before all things". (*Col* 1:15-20)

- Messianic, redeeming sacrifice:
  It was Yahweh's good pleasure to crush him with pain;
  If he gives his life as a sin offering,
  He will see his offspring and prolong his life,
  And through him Yahweh's good pleasure will be done.
  (*Is* 53:11)

The tradition I handed on to you [*paradidomi*] in the
first place, a tradition which I had myself received
[*paralambanomai*], was that Christ died for our sins,
in accordance with the scriptures, and that he was
buried; and that on the third day, he was raised to life, in
accordance with the scriptures; and that he appeared to
Cephas; and later to the Twelve; and next he appeared
to more than five hundred of the brothers at the same
time. (*1 Co* 15:3-6)

Interestingly, the bracketed words above indicate word
for word teaching - in effect learning by heart a set text or
statement of belief. They refer to the teaching Paul received
in Jerusalem a very few years after the crucifixion. Thus
even at such an early date, the Church had formulated a

standard set of beliefs about Jesus's saving sacrifice for each of us.

- Unique place of God to forgive sins, perform miracles, receive worship:

  See now that I, I am He, And beside me there is no other God. It is I who deal death and life; When I have struck, it is I who heal (no one can rescue anyone from me). (*Dt* 32:39)

  Peter said [to the beggar crippled from birth], "I have neither silver nor gold, but I will give you what I have: in the name of Jesus Christ the Nazarene, walk!" (*Ac* 3:1-9)

  As they were stoning him, Stephen said in invocation, "Lord Jesus, receive my spirit". Then he knelt down and said aloud, "Lord, do not hold this sin against them". (*Ac* 7:59)

  Wherefore, so that I should not get above myself, I was given a thorn in the flesh… About this, I have three times pleaded with the Lord that it might leave me; but he has answered me, "My grace is enough for you: for power is at full stretch in weakness." It is, then, about my weakness that I am happiest of all to boast, so that the power of Christ may rest upon me…" (*2 Cor* 12:7-10).

The prophet Joel looks to the new age, the day of Yahweh and the outpouring of the Spirit: "All who call on the name of Yahweh will be saved" (*Joel* 3:5). In Romans, Paul quotes a ritual acclamation, a part of worship, using similar words but referring to Jesus: "...if you declare with your mouth that Jesus is Lord, and if you believe with your heart that God raised him from the dead, then you will be saved. (*Rm* 10:9,10)

The judgement of history

How many divisions does the Pope of Rome have?
(Joseph Stalin)[25]

Truth is the daughter of time. So what has time proved of the Church? Immediately after the Resurrection, the group of followers was tiny - only the Apostles (and the women who witnessed the Resurrection). In the period of forty days between Resurrection and Ascension, the disciples saw and spoke with Jesus, were instructed and grew in faith and understanding. The group grew to about 120. At Pentecost (about seven weeks after the crucifixion) Peter made his inspired address to the crowds, and three thousand became believers (*Ac* 2:41). The rapid expansion continued, and soon there were five thousand believers (*Ac* 4:4). By the seventh century AD, *Acts* 2 reports that believers numbered "many thousands".

Persecution and growth

Persecution started early. Stephen was martyred about two to three years after the crucifixion. Christians dispersed, and preached in new cities and countries, both to Jews and Gentiles. Indeed, the disciples were first given the name "Christians" in Antioch (*Ac* 11:26). Luke emphasises in Acts the openness of the new faith to believers of other nations and backgrounds - including an Ethiopian eunuch - a high ranking state official (*Ac* 8:27); a Jew from Tarsus (Turkey) - Saul (*Ac* 9:1); and a Gentile centurion from Rome - Cornelius (*Ac* 10:1).

Onto this scene comes the dramatic figure of Saul, later Paul. He was converted after receiving a vision of Jesus (and hearing Jesus's words) while on a journey to Damascus to persecute Christians. He was struck blind, travelled on to Damascus and spent three days fasting, praying and meditating. On the third day a Christian named Ananias interpreted his revelation for him; he regained his sight and was baptised (*Ac* 9, 10-19). All this occurred not long after the crucifixion - perhaps three or four years afterwards.

Paul then spent time (perhaps three years) in Arabia, meditating on his new understanding; returned to Jerusalem and stayed with Peter, James and John (*Ga* 1:18, 19); and then embarked on his various missionary journeys - Cyprus, Malta, Turkey, Greece, Rome, possibly Spain. The spread of Christianity was extraordinarily fast: "Within thirty or forty years after the death of Jesus, every major city of Asia Minor, Greece and Italy had one or more Christian congregations".[26] This growth occurred notwithstanding periodic and savage persecution. James the Greater was martyred in AD 44 (*Ac* 12:1, 2), James the Just, leader of the Jerusalem Christians, was martyred in AD 62 or 69. The Emperor Nero conducted a major persecution of Christians after the disastrous fire in Rome in AD 64. Further persecutions flared up from time to time: in Asia in AD 166 (when Polycarp was martyred); under Maximus Thrax (AD 238); under Decius (AD 249-251); the Valerian persecution of AD 258; then the Great Persecution under Diocletian from AD 303. Eventually, Christianity was legalised under Constantine 1 in AD 313.

The Church in the modern world

The persecution of Christians has, of course, continued throughout history. It has been episodic, sometimes more and sometimes less vigorous. It continues today. In the last century, it occurred in communist Russia, Mexico, China, Nazi Germany. In current times it continues in many Muslim dominated countries. According to the World Evangelical Alliance, over 200 million Christians are denied fundamental human rights solely because of their faith. Pope Benedict XVI stated that Christians are the most persecuted group in the contemporary world. Yet the faith grows. Paradoxically, it springs up, more vigorous than ever, in countries where it has been persecuted. It is the largest faith group in the world, with 2.8 billion followers - nearly a third of the global population. In Russia, where state repression only ended with the fall of communism, over half the population describes itself as Christian. In China, where Christianity was heavily repressed for much of the twentieth century, and where the state still seeks to regulate the Church, it is estimated that there may be

100 million (or even more) Christians, and the Church is growing very rapidly.

An extraordinary story. Empire after empire has risen, flourished and declined; the politically and militarily powerful, the formidable, the "opinion formers" have determined to eliminate Christianity, and used great power, cruelty and subtlety to do so. Yet now we see over a third of the world's population as Christian, while those persecuting empires are long withered away, the powerful persecutors vanished, their bodies to dust, their souls to judgement.

Conclusions

For man cannot be fully understood without Christ. Or rather, man is incapable of understanding himself fully without Christ. He cannot understand who he is, nor what his true dignity is, nor what his vocation is, nor what his final end is. He cannot understand any of this without Christ.

(Pope John Paul II)[27]

A cloud of doubt, blown by the winds of culture, hangs over us. Can it really be so? Does God really exist? Is Jesus God? The evidence that says "Yes" is powerful; and yet, and yet - we pause; we hesitate. Can such a staggering, vast, extraordinary thing be true?

Do we choose to believe, or do we choose not? That is a real choice, and it must be so, to preserve our fundamental freedom. We are given much evidence and encouragement; but we are not compelled.

We will feel doubt at times. In those times, our reason and knowledge can help. So can the report of others. So can the recollection of our deep experiences of faith: the occasions when we saw, and knew certainty. Those experiences are not to be downgraded by the passage of time. The quality they held when we passed through them is unchanging.

We have reviewed the evidence. Yes, Jesus lived; yes, he said and did extraordinary things; yes, eyewitnesses and contemporaries were convinced, changed their lives, accepted denial, suffering, and martyrdom to follow him and proclaim that he is one with God, shares the nature and powers of God, is properly worshipped as God; yes, he was resurrected; yes, he appeared to many after his resurrection, walked, ate, spoke, but also had particular powers - to pass through walls, to vanish; yes, there are countless examples of miracles performed in his name, prayers to him answered.

In light of all that, to seek to make our peace with doubt by saying: "A wonderful man, a marvellous teacher, a man of extraordinary wisdom, courage and power," and pause there, is a response of weakness. It ignores the detailed evidence. It yields to embarrassment, flinching from a conclusion cutting across much popular culture and received wisdom in Britain today.

Ill winds will press upon our judgement. But in our hearts, and in our intellect, we know better. We cannot understand ourselves, our world, our destiny, without Christ. We cannot find touch with reality until we acknowledge the truth. The evidence is clear: Jesus is one of the three persons of the Trinity. Jesus is God.

Bibliography

Hall, Richard *Brilliant Presentation*

Catechism of the Catholic Church

Ehrman, Bart D., *Did Jesus Exist: The Historical Arguments for Jesus of Nazareth*

McDowell, Josh and Wilson, Bill, *He Walked Among Us*

Kenyon, Sir Frederic, *Our Bible and The Ancient Manuscripts* (revised edition, 1958)

Leach, Charles, *Our Bible, How We Got It*

Ratzinger, Cardinal Joseph, *Seven Theses on Christology and the Hermeneutic of Faith*

Holloway, Julia Bolton (translator), *Showing of Love: Julian of Norwich*

Howse, Christopher (ed.), *The Best Sermons Ever*

Strobel, Lee, *The Case for Christ*

Overman, Dean, *The Case for the Divinity of Christ*

Blomberg, Craig L., *The Historical Reliability of the Gospels*

Kempis, Thomas à, *The Imitation of Christ*

McDowell, Josh, *The New Evidence That Demands a Verdict*

Bruce, F.F., *The New Testament Documents: Are They Reliable?*

Metzger, Bruce M., *The New Testament: It's Background, Growth and Content*

Bunyan, John, *The Pilgrim's Progress*

Further reading

Fermor, Patrick Leigh, *A Time to Keep Silence*

Lewis, C.S., *Christian Reflections*

Hurtado, Larry, *Lord Jesus Christ*

Rivers, Scott, *No Man is an Island: A Selection from the Prose of John Donne*

Pascal, Blaise, *Pensees*

Bowman jr, Robert M. and Komoszewski, J. Ed, *Putting Jesus in His Place*

Merton, Thomas, *Seasons of Celebration*

Strobel, Lee, *The Case for the Real Jesus*

Boros, Fr L., *The Moment of Truth*

Betz, Otto, *What Do We Know About Jesus*

Acknowledgements

A number of people were kind enough to help me with their comments. I would like to thank in particular Antony Pugh Thomas, Richard Stones and Pauline Watford. Their contributions were enormously helpful and very much appreciated. However, the contents of this booklet should not be taken to reflect their views.

Endnotes

[1] Extract from the translation of the Nicene Creed used in the order of Mass. The Creed was adopted at the council of Nicea in AD 325, and updated at the Council of Constantinople in AD 381. It is widely used in Christian celebrations of all denominations.

[2] Bart D. Ehrman, *Did Jesus Exist? The Historical Argument for Jesus of Nazareth.*

[3] Translation from Josh McDowell and Bill Wilson, *He Walked Among Us.*

[4] Translation from Bruce M. Metzger (1914-2007), *The New Testament: Its Background, Growth and Content.*

[5] Translation from Josh McDowell, *The New Evidence That Demands a Verdict.*

[6] Translation from Bruce M. Metzger, *The New Testament: Its Background, Growth and Content.*

[7] Translation from Josh McDowell: *The New Evidence That Demands a Verdict*.

[8] F.F. Bruce (1910-1990), *The New Testament Documents: Are They Reliable?*

[9] Bart D. Ehrman, *Did Jesus Exist? The Historical Argument for Jesus of Nazareth*.

[10] *Dei Verbum,* quoted in the *Catechism of the Catholic Church*, *126.

[11] Translation from Craig L. Blomberg, *The Historical Reliability of the Gospels*.

[12] Translation from Josh McDowell, *The New Evidence That Demands a Verdict*.

[13] Bruce M. Metzger (1914-2007), *The New Testament: Its Background, Growth and Content*.

[14] Sir Frederic Kenyon (1863-1952), *Our Bible and the Ancient Manuscripts*.

[15] F.F. Bruce, *The New Testament Documents: Are They Reliable?*

[16] Citing C. Leach (1847-1919), *Our Bible, How We Got It* 145.

[17] Craig L. Blomberg (1914-2007), *The Historical Reliability of the Gospels*.

[18] Thomas à Kempis (1379-1471), *The Imitation of Christ*.

[19] Richard Hall, *Brilliant Presentation*.

[20] Cardinal Ratzinger (later Pope Benedict XVI), *Seven Theses on Christology and the Hermeneutic of Faith*.

[21] John Locke (1632-1704), *An Essay Concerning Human Understanding*.

[2] Julian of Norwich (c. 1342-1416), *Showing of Love*.

[23] John Bunyan (1628-1688), *The Pilgrim's Progress*.

[24] Dean L. Overman, *The Case for the Divinity of Jesus*.

[25] Joseph Stalin (1879-1953).

[26] Bruce M. Metzger, *The New Testament: Its Background, Growth and Content*.

[27] Pope John Paul II (1920-2005), *Sermon in Victory Square*, Warsaw, 1979.